The Right Place for Jupiter

Story by Sonny Mulheron

Illustrations by Mary Ann Hurley

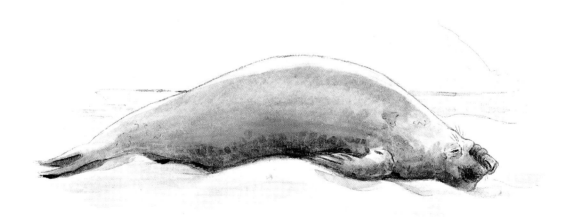

One summer morning, a huge elephant seal swam into a busy harbor. He was looking for a sheltered beach.

Soon he found just the right place. He heaved himself up onto the sand, and flopped down in the sun by a seawall. Then he closed his eyes and went to sleep.

2

The beach was near the heart of a city. People who lived in the apartments and houses pointed at the enormous animal. Children stared over the seawall in amazement. Most people had never seen an elephant seal before, but here was one, on a city beach, close enough to touch!

Soon cars and people crowded all the nearby streets, causing major traffic jams.

Most people just wanted to stand and look, but a few of them wouldn't leave the elephant seal alone. Someone tried to feed him ice cream. One man poked him with a stick, and then someone else threw a stone at him. The elephant seal snorted, but he didn't budge.

It wasn't long before the police arrived to move the cars along. Then two officers pushed their way through the crowds and went down the steps onto the beach.

"Jumping Jupiter!" said one of them. "I've never seen anything like that on the beach before!"

"He may be Jupiter," replied the other officer, "but he's certainly not jumping. Perhaps he's ill."

"Move back, please," he ordered. "Don't annoy him!"

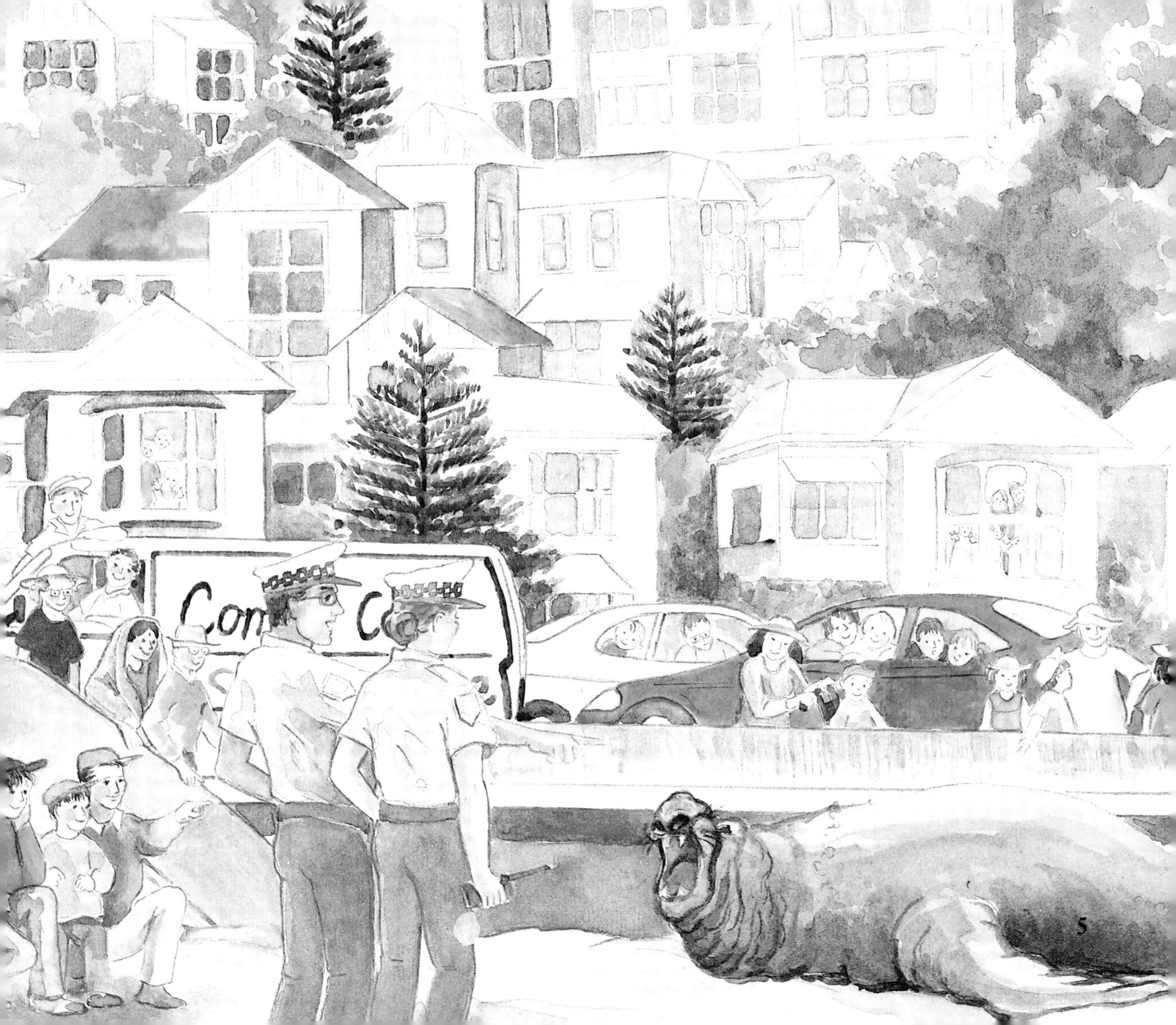

The police officer called a professor at the university. "How do we move an elephant seal?" he asked.

"Why can't you leave him where he is?" said the professor.

"Because he's lying on a city beach," replied the police officer. "He could be ill, and someone has been throwing stones!"

"We can't allow that," said the professor. "But I don't think that he's ill. He's probably ready to molt," she explained. "He just needs a place to rest while his old fur falls out. I'll come and take a look. Male elephant seals all come ashore this time of the year, and stay for a couple of months."

"A couple of months! He can't stay **here** that long!" said the police officer. "Jupiter has picked the wrong beach."

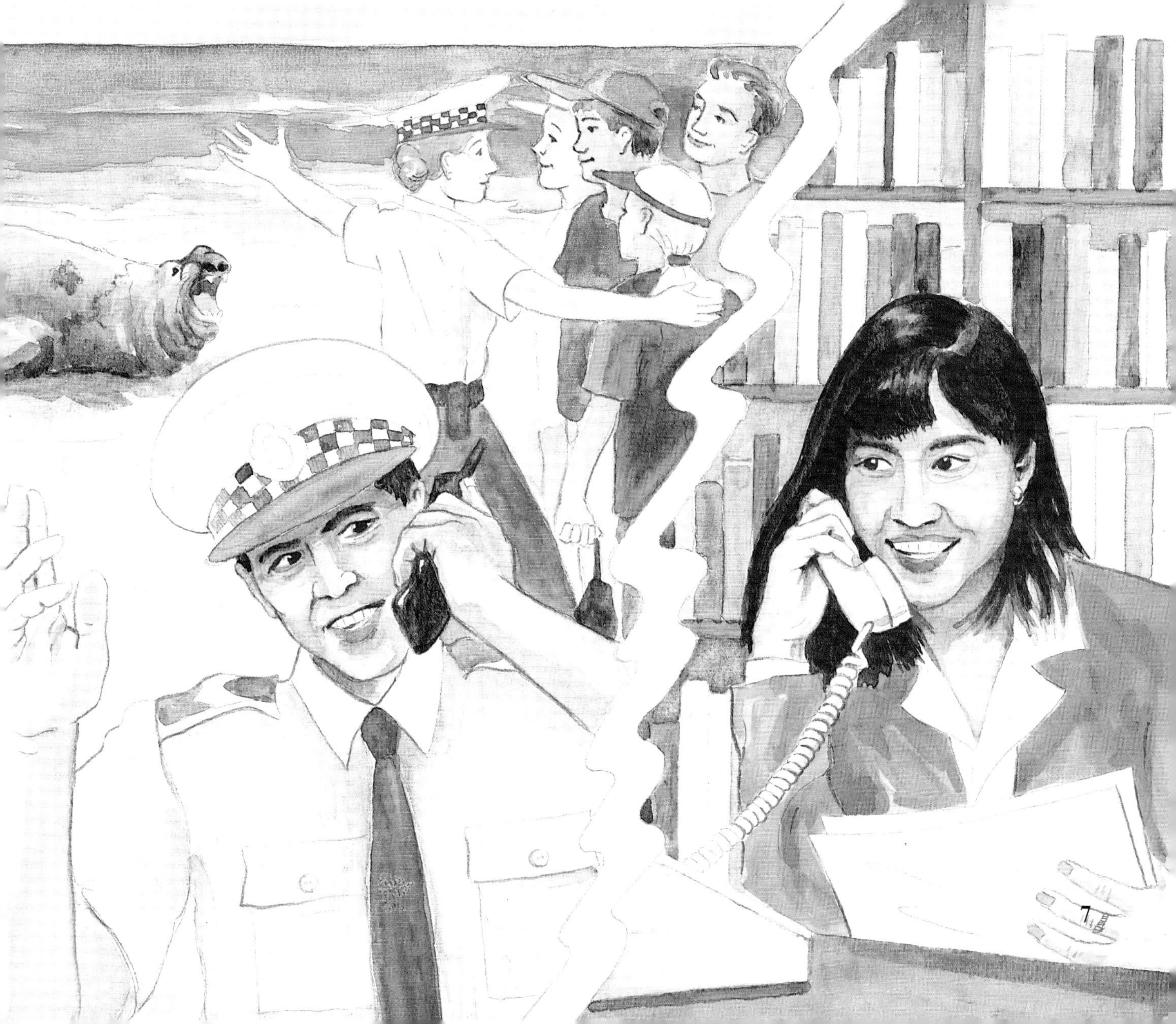

The professor came to look at Jupiter. "I'm sure he has come here to molt," she said. "If we can get him back in the water, he might move to a different beach — one outside the harbor."

"I'll call the harbormaster," said the police officer.

The harbormaster sent some people with a net, but Jupiter was so heavy, they couldn't move him.

More workers came, with a bigger net. They threw it over Jupiter and dragged him into the sea. But as soon as he reached the water, he slipped out of the net and waddled up the beach again, and there he stayed.

Jupiter was an elephant seal with a mind of his own. A television crew came to film him, and his picture was printed on the front page of the paper.

Jupiter wins!
Elephant seal won't go

Because Jupiter was in the news, the crowds and the traffic jams grew bigger than ever.

So the harbormaster sent along a boat with a large crane. "This time we'll hoist him aboard in the net and take him well outside the harbor," he told the police. "That will work."

But by now, Jupiter knew about nets, and he didn't like them. As soon as he saw the workers coming with the net, he heaved himself down into the water. He swam out to sea a little way and watched. When the workers took the net away, he came back!

The workers tried three times, but Jupiter wouldn't let them come anywhere near him.

Jupiter wins again, said the headline. It was true. An elephant seal had outwitted all the experts!

Jupiter wins again

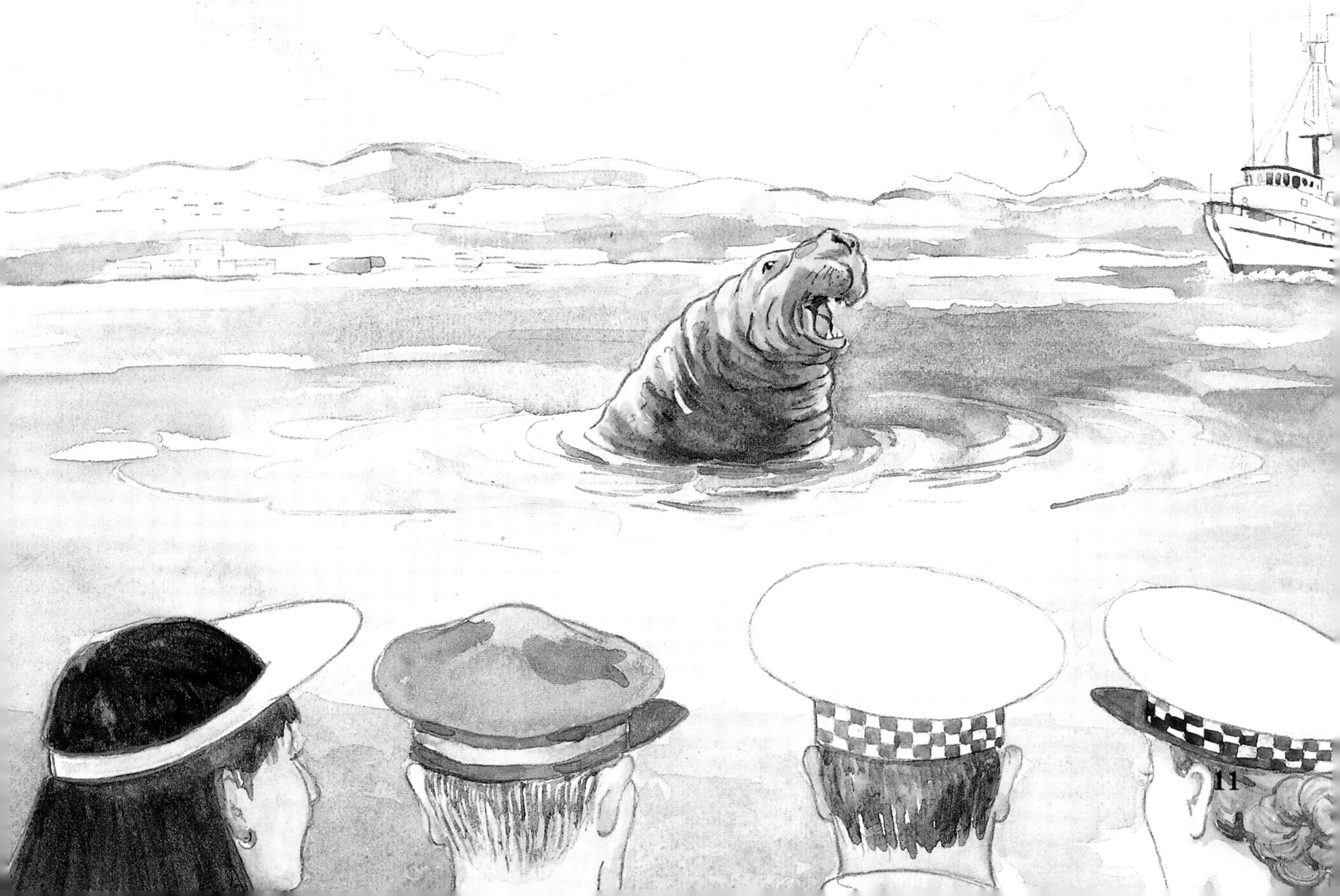

They called a meeting.

"It's no use trying to move Jupiter again," said the professor. "Even if you did manage to take him out to sea, he's likely to come back."

"Then we must make sure that no one harms him," said the woman from Animal Welfare. "That means we'll have to find babysitters to guard him, day and night."

"We'll build a rope fence around him," said the harbormaster.

"We'll keep someone on patrol," said the police.

But when the fence went up, Jupiter flipped it down with his tail. It looked too much like the nets! It had to be built farther away so that he didn't feel trapped.

Then Jupiter wriggled himself more comfortably into the sand and went to sleep.

And there he stayed for eight long weeks. Jupiter dozed the time away, and ate nothing. His babysitters stayed on guard, day after day. Television crews filmed him several times, and visitors came from distant places. Everyone loved him.

Jupiter was famous. He was molting where **he** wanted to molt, right in the middle of the city beach!

Slowly Jupiter's old brown hair and skin fell off. He looked very odd, with ragged pieces hanging down from his back and sides.

15

But when summer was over, all his ragged fur had gone. Jupiter's new coat was smooth and shiny. He sat up and sniffed the sea. His eyes were bright. He arched his back and wriggled his flippers. Then he waddled down the beach and slipped through the waves into deep water. He flicked his tail and headed for the fishing grounds in the ocean.

His tired babysitters cheered. Jupiter, in his brand new coat, was back in the sea where he belonged.